Seeing Both Sides

Class Parties, Yes or No

Reese Everett

Educational Media

rourkeeducationalmedia.com

Scan for Related Titles
and Teacher Resources

Before Reading:

Building Academic Vocabulary and Background Knowledge

Before reading a book, it is important to tap into what your child or students already know about the topic. This will help them develop their vocabulary, increase their reading comprehension, and make connections across the curriculum.

1. *Look at the cover of the book. What will this book be about?*
2. *What do you already know about the topic?*
3. *Let's study the Table of Contents. What will you learn about in the book's chapters?*
4. *What would you like to learn about this topic? Do you think you might learn about it from this book? Why or why not?*
5. *Use a reading journal to write about your knowledge of this topic. Record what you already know about the topic and what you hope to learn about the topic.*
6. *Read the book.*
7. *In your reading journal, record what you learned about the topic and your response to the book.*
8. *After reading the book complete the activities below.*

Content Area Vocabulary
Read the list. What do these words mean?

alternative
attentive
beliefs
burden
community
consume
discouraged
diversity
hazard
insincerity
oppose
support
traditions

After Reading:

Comprehension and Extension Activity

After reading the book, work on the following questions with your child or students in order to check their level of reading comprehension and content mastery.

1. *What is an opinion? (Summarize)*
2. *Explain why two people might have the same opinion for different reasons. (Infer)*
3. *What are some ways parties can teach you about other cultures? (Asking questions)*
4. *How does being in school on your birthday make you feel? (Text to self connection)*
5. *What are some reasons holiday parties at school aren't a good idea? (Asking questions)*

Extension Activity
Plan a party for your class. Write down everything you'll need. Then check the prices for each item at the store or online. Tally up the total amount you'd need to spend to provide all the items for the entire class. How much will your party cost?

Table of Contents

Taking Sides

When you're a student, you spend a lot of time at school. You develop friendships with your classmates, and may want to celebrate special occasions with them.

In some schools, class parties are allowed. In others, they are **discouraged**.

What do you think about parties at school? What information do you have that supports your opinion?

An opinion is someone's belief based on their experiences and the information available to them. People can have different opinions about an issue. Sometimes people change their minds when they look at something from another point of view.

Let's look at arguments that **support** and **oppose** class parties. Then you can decide.

Parties in Class? Yes, Please!

School should be more than just a place to learn about history, math, and science. It should be a place students enjoy spending their time: a place where they can get to know their friends and have some fun now and then.

Reality ✓

Students in the United States spend about 180 days in school each year.

School should not be all work and no play. Everyone needs some down time. Why not have a party to celebrate a holiday or a success?

Taking time to celebrate special occasions in the classroom is a great way to bring students, teachers, and families together.

7

Many students' birthdays occur on a school day. They should be allowed to celebrate–at least a little bit! Sharing treats with the class is a fun way to make a student feel special.

Reality ✓

Some birthday treats may not be okay for everyone because of allergies or health concerns. Providing an **alternative** treat for these students allows everyone to participate in the party.

Some students may want to stay home from school on their birthday. Allowing birthday parties in the classroom could make them think twice about that. A missed school day is a lost opportunity to learn. Celebrating birthdays in the classroom can keep students from skipping school.

Class parties are an excellent way to encourage and reward good behavior. If students know they will earn a pizza or ice cream party for staying on task throughout each school day, they may be more focused. When everyone in class is **attentive** every day, more learning happens.

Students who miss a party because of negative behavior may be motivated to make positive changes. Missing out on the fun is no fun at all. Celebrating good behavior is rewarding for students and teachers, not just on the day of the party, but every day it encourages positive actions.

Reality ✓

Experts say positive reinforcement, such as rewards for good behavior, can help children learn.

Many people look forward to celebrating holidays, whether it's Thanksgiving, Martin Luther King Day, Hanukah, or Christmas. Sometimes all the students in a classroom celebrate the same holidays. Sometimes they don't. But that's okay. Holiday parties provide opportunities to learn about different cultures, religions, and **traditions**.

Students from different backgrounds can learn from each other by sharing holiday foods, games, and stories. Just because a student may not celebrate a particular holiday doesn't mean they can't enjoy the party and learn something new. Class parties are a fun, relaxed setting for students to develop an appreciation for **diversity** at school and in the world.

In addition, class holiday parties can boost students' skills and confidence. For example, Halloween parties give students an opportunity to use their creative skills to design costumes and decorations. Valentine's Day parties give students a chance to tell their classmates what they admire about them.

Inviting family members to attend class holiday parties allows them to interact with other parents and students. The families get to celebrate with their student, meet new people, and learn something new. This brings people together and promotes a sense of school **community**.

Reality ✓

Family involvement at school promotes better grades and behavior.

Class parties can be used to support learning and positive behavior. They can help students get to know each other. They can bring families together. They are not just a break from teaching and learning, classroom parties can be educational for everyone.

Parties at School? No Way!

There is a time to work and a time to play. In school, time in the classroom should be spent learning. Allowing parties during class time takes away from instruction and creates distractions.

Celebrating special occasions is important, but those celebrations should take place outside of school.

Reality ✓

Only 180 days a year are spent in school. That leaves 185 days for celebrating holidays and birthdays outside the classroom.

Teachers, students, and parents have a lot to do and a lot to keep up with already. Planning a class party is an extra **burden** on everyone. Parents are expected to buy or bake treats. They may be expected to buy paper goods, such as plates and napkins, for the class.

Teachers may also be expected to provide treats and materials for party activities. Some parents and teachers may not be able to afford to buy things for a class party. It isn't fair to ask them to spend money for things that are not necessary for learning.

Reality ✓

Teachers spend about $500 of their own money on back-to-school supplies each year.

Some students and parents enjoy providing birthday treats for everyone in the class. But other families may not have the time or the money to provide items for a classroom celebration. Students who do not get a class party because their families cannot afford it may feel badly.

Even if everyone in a class could bring in treats, celebrating each student's birthday at school takes a lot of time! If every student celebrated their birthday with a classroom party, that could end up being 20 to 30 or more parties a year.

Reality ✓

Twenty 30-minute parties per school year would take up 10 hours of learning time.

Holiday parties are also a bad idea for schools. Students come from diverse backgrounds. If you're going to celebrate the holidays of one culture, to be fair you must celebrate them all. If you have a party for every holiday, you lose class time and spend a lot of money.

Some students' religious **beliefs** may prevent them from participating in a holiday party. They must be excused from class during the celebration. They may feel left out and sad. They also are missing out on learning during the time the rest of the class is attending the party.

Reality ✓

In the U.S., students and teachers do not have to participate in activities that are contrary to their religious beliefs.

Parties for Valentine's Day can make students feel awkward or uncomfortable because they have to give out sentimental cards to everyone in class. Halloween parties can scare young students with creepy decorations and costumes. It is best to not have these parties at all to avoid any problems.

Reality ✓

Making students give a Valentine's Day card to everyone in class can confuse the idea of meaningful gift-giving and may encourage **insincerity.**

When one class has a party, it can be distracting for students in other classrooms. The noise can make it difficult for them to pay attention. Those students may feel it is unfair that they are working while other students are not.

What do people eat at parties? Chips, cake, and ice cream come to mind. Unhealthy foods should never be provided at school. Some students are not allowed to eat junk food. Some have allergies that prevent them from eating certain things. It is not fair to these students to have food in the classroom that they cannot **consume**.

Reality ✓

Allowing foods in the classroom can cause a safety hazard for students with severe allergies.

Classroom parties are an added expense that students' families and teachers don't need. Parents and teachers already have to spend money on supplies. They shouldn't have to worry about parties, too. Classroom parties are time-consuming and distracting. They do not improve students' success in school, so they should not be a part of the school day.

Your Turn

What do you think about class parties now that you've read arguments from both sides? Each side supported their opinion with facts and examples. Which side had the strongest points?

Think about your position on this issue, then write about your opinion using facts and examples. You may want to mention your own classroom experiences.

Telling Your Side: Writing Opinion Pieces

- Tell your opinion first. Use phrases such as:
- *I like* _____.
- *I think* _____.
- _____ *is the best* _____.
- Give multiple reasons to support your opinion. Use facts and relevant information instead of stating your feelings.
- Use the words *and*, *because*, and *also* to connect your opinion to your reasons.
- Clarify or explain your facts by using the phrases *for example* or *such as*.
- Compare your opinion to a different opinion. Then point out reasons that your opinion is better. You can use phrases such as:
- *Some people think* _____, *but I disagree because* _____.
- _____ *is better than* _____ *because* _____.
- Give examples of positive outcomes if the reader agrees with your opinion. For example, you can use the phrase, *If* _____ *then* _____.
- Use a personal story about your own experiences with your topic. For example, if you are writing about your opinion on after-school sports, you can write about your own experiences with after-school sports activities.
- Finish your opinion piece with a strong conclusion that highlights your strongest arguments. Restate your opinion so your reader remembers how you feel.

Glossary

alternative (awl-TUR-nuh-tive): different

attentive (uh-TEN-tiv): alert and paying close attention

beliefs (bi-LEEFS): ideas that form someone's religion

burden (BUR-duhn): a heavy load or serious responsibility

community (kuh-MYOO-ni-tee): a group of people who have
something in common

consume (kuhn-SOOM): to eat or drink something

discouraged (dis-KUR-ijd): feeling less confident or
enthusiastic

diversity (di-VUR-si-tee): a variety

hazard (HAZ-urd): something that is dangerous or likely to
cause problems

insincerity (in-sin-SER-i-tee): not genuine or honest

oppose (uh- POZE): disagree with something or someone

support (suh-PORT): to be in favor of something

traditions (truh-DISH-uhns): customs, ideas and beliefs
handed down from one generation to the next

Index

Show What You Know

1. What is the difference between a fact and an opinion?

2. How many days do most students spend in school each year?

3. Why might class parties be unfair for some students?

4. What are the benefits of celebrating a variety of holidays in school?

5. Can parties at school be dangerous for some students? Explain.

Websites to Visit

www.timeforkids.com/homework-helper/a-plus-papers/
   persuasive-essay

www.readwritethink.org/files/resources/interactives/persuasion_map

http://pbskids.org/arthur/games/factsopinions/index.html

About the Author

Reese Everett is an author, editor, and journalist from Tampa, Florida. She is also a mother of four kids who think every day should include some kind of party. It's Tuesday and it's pouring rain? Party on!

Meet The Author!
www.meetREMauthors.com

www.rourkeeducationalmedia.com

PHOTO CREDITS: Cover (top), page 3: ©Globalstock; page 1, 14: ©Rodolfo Arguedas; page 4: ©Derek Latta; page 7: ©7nuit; page 6: ©Dankloff; page 7: ©Darrin Henry Photography; page 7, 8, 11, 15, 17, 19, 21, 23, 24, 26: ©loops7; page 8: ©Rafal Stachura; page 9: ©IPGGutenbergUKLtd; page 10: ©RichLegs; page 11: ©jane; page 12: ©Brian McEntire; page 13: ©Lisa F. Young; page 15: ©Steve Debenport; page 16: ©Susan Chiang; page 17: ©artisteer; page 18: ©Aldo Murillo; page 19: ©YinYang; page 20, 25: ©MonkeyBusinessImages; page 21: ©DenisNata; page 22: ©STILLFX; page 23: ©CatLondon; page 24: ©auleena; page 26: ©Joe_Potato; page 27: ©dosecreative; page 28: ©Yuri Arcurs; page 29: ©Sezeryadigar

Edited by: Keli Sipperley

Cover design and Interior design by: Rhea Magaro

Library of Congress PCN Data

Class Parties, Yes or No / Reese Everett
 (Seeing Both Sides)
 ISBN 978-1-68191-383-4 (hard cover)
 ISBN 978-1-68191-425-1(soft cover)
 ISBN 978-1-68191-465-7(e-Book)
Library of Congress Control Number: 2015951550

Also Available as:

ROURKE'S
e-Books

Printed in the United States of America, North Mankato, Minnesota